817.5
Bombe
Eat l
 more

D0175060

MID-CONTINENT PUBLIC LIBRARY
North Oak Branch
8700 N. Oak Trafficway **NO**
Kansas City, MO 64155

WITHDRAWN
FROM THE RECORDS OF THE
MID-CONTINENT PUBLIC LIBRARY

_To:_ _____

From: _____

Eat Less Cottage Cheese and More Ice Cream

and

More Ice Cream

Thoughts on Life from Erma Bombeck

Andrews McMeel Publishing

Kansas City

Eat Less Cottage Cheese and More Ice Cream copyright © 1979, 2003 by Erma Bombeck. All rights reserved. Printed in Singapore. No part of this book may be used or reproduced in any manner whatsoever without written permission except in the case of reprints in the context of reviews. For information, write Andrews McMeel Publishing, an Andrews McMeel Universal company, 4520 Main Street, Kansas City, Missouri 64111.

03 04 05 06 07 TWP 10 9 8 7 6 5 4 3 2 1

ISBN: 0-7407-2127-5

Library of Congress Control Number: 2002113733

Illustrations by Lynn Chang

The text of this book originally appeared in a newspaper column, "If I Had My Life to Live Over," on December 2, 1979.

ATTENTION SCHOOLS AND BUSINESSES

Andrews McMeel books are available at quantity discounts with bulk purchase for educational, business, or sales promotional use. For information, please write to: Special Sales Department, Andrews McMeel Publishing, 4520 Main Street, Kansas City, Missouri 64111.

MID-CONTINENT PUBLIC LIBRARY

3 0000 12455456 3

MID-CONTINENT PUBLIC LIBRARY
North Oak Branch
8700 N. Oak Trafficway
Kansas City, MO 64155

NO

Eat Less
Cottage Cheese
and
More Ice Cream

Someone asked me **the other day** *if I had my life to live over,* would I change anything.

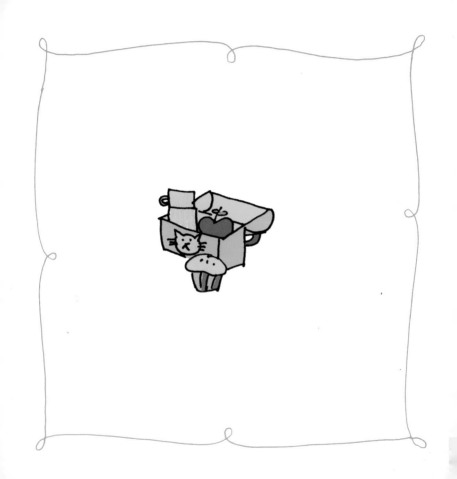

My answer was no, but then I *thought* about it and **changed** m y m i n d .

If I had my
life to live
over again
I would have
talked less
and
listened more.

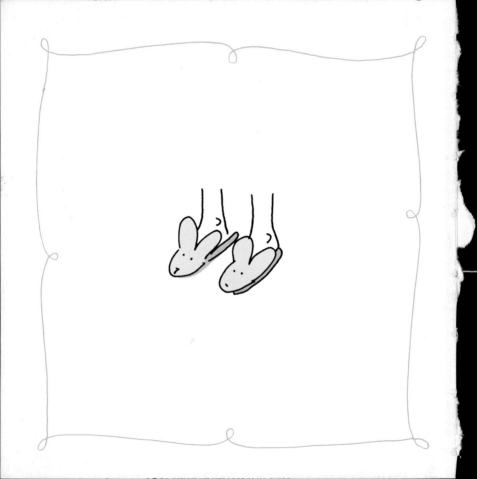

*Instead of
wishing away
nine months
of pregnancy and
complaining about
the shadow over my feet,
I'd have cherished every minute
of it and realized that the wonderment
growing inside me was to be my only
chance in life to assist **God** in a miracle.*

I would never have
insisted the car windows
be rolled up on a summer day
because my hair had just been
teased and SPRAYED.

I would have invited
friends over to
dinner even if the
carpet was **stained**
and the sofa faded.

I would have eaten

p o p c o r n in the "good"

living room and

worried **less** about

the dirt when

you lit the

fireplace.

I would have
taken the time
to listen to my
grandfather
ramble about
his youth.

I would have burnt

the pink *candle*

that was sculptured

like a rose before it

melted in storage.

I would
have sat
CROSS-LEGGED

on the lawn
with my children
and never worried
about grass stains.

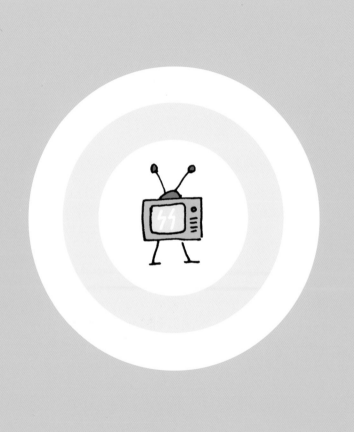

I would have

cried and *laughed*

less

while watching television . . . and

more

while watching real life.

I would
have shared
more of the
responsibility
carried by
my husband.

I would have eaten less
cottage cheese
and more
ice cream.

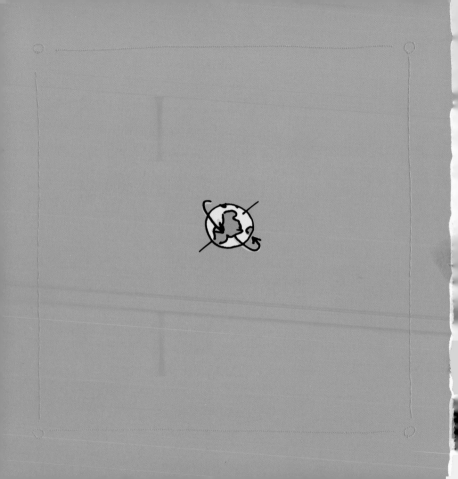

I would have **gone to** **bed** when I was **sick** instead of *pretending* the Earth would go into a holding pattern if I weren't there for a day.

 I would
never have
bought *anything*
just because it
was practical/wouldn't
show soil/was guaran-
teed to last a lifetime.

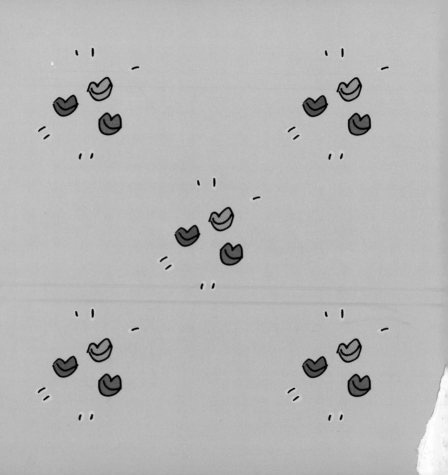

When my child kissed me

impetuously,

I would never have said,

"Later.

Now go get washed up for dinner."

There would
have been more
I love yous . . .
more I'm sorrys . . .
more I'm listenings . . .

but **mostly,**
given another shot
at *life,*
I would seize
every minute of it . . .

look at it

and

really

see

it . . .

try it on ...

live it ...

exhaus

it ...

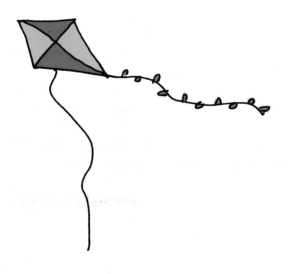

and

never

give that minute back

until there was

nothing left

of it.